KWANZAA

by Melrose Cooper

illustrated by Dawn W. Majewski

ISBN: 1-58521-002-1

Published by: BBC Inc., P.O. Box 13261, Reading, PA 19612-3261

KWANZAA!

by Melrose Cooper

illustrated by Dawn W. Majewski

Contents

Everywhere

Food is on the table,
Our feast's about to start.
There's rumbling in my tummy
And Kwanzaa in my heart.

Kinaras in the windows,
Benderas on the air,
There's love and light and friendship.
It's Kwanzaa everywhere!

[11] *Kwanzaa (KWAHN zah) is a holiday that celebrates African American culture, history, and customs. The word comes from the Kiswahili (kee swah HEE lee) language and means "first fruits of harvest time." The holiday was begun in 1966 by a teacher, Dr. Maulana Karenga.*

A kinara (kee NAH rah) is the candle holder that has spaces for seven candles – three red, three green, and one black.

A bendera (ben DEHR ah) is the flag of three horizontal stripes (red on top, black in the middle, green at the bottom) that was designed by Marcus Garvey and is used during Kwanzaa.

Corn Count

Wake, awake to Kwanzaa
This December morn.
Spread out the mkeka;
Get the ears of corn.
For the kids a-coming,
Set out one apiece.
Two are for my cousins,
Charmaine and Cherise.
Three are for my brothers,
Noah, Josh, and Seth.
Two more for our neighbors,
Alima and Beth.
Two more for my best friends,
Janie and Tyree.
Oops, now how could I forget?
I need one more for me![2]

[2] *A mkeka (em KEE kah) is a placemat used on a Kwanzaa table. One ear of corn is placed on top of it to represent each child who will attend the celebration. The name for this "Kwanzaa corn" is muhindi (moo HIN dee).*

Alima (Ah lee mah) is a name from North Africa which means "wise."

The Colors of Kwanzaa

There are three colors of Kwanzaa.
The first of these colors is red,
A symbol for all the struggles,
The blood that our people have shed.

Green is the color that stands for
The lush, living African land
And for all the justice and fairness
We're working to have close at hand.

Black is the color for People,
For all of the folks in the race
And for the lustre and richness
Of my own beautiful face.

Nguzo Saba

Seven guiding principles,
Seven shining lights
Showing us the way by day
Brighening our nights.

Each of seven magic words
Gleaming like a star,
Helping us to celebrate
Who and what we are.
3

[3]The Nguzo Saba (en GOO zoh tsah bah) are the seven principles of
Kwanzaa. One of them is highlighed during each of the seven days of
celebration.
The names for these principles are:
1, Umoja (oo MOO jah) – unity
2. Kujichagulia (KOO jee chah goo LEE ah) – control of oneself
3. Ujima (oo JEE mah) –cooperation
4. Ujamaa (oo jah MAH) – sharing profits; buying from each other
5. Nia (NEE ah) – purpose
6. Kuumba (koo OOM bah) – creativity
7. Imani (ee MAH nee) –faith [v3]

Unity

I'm not too crazy about Lamar,
And Jessica bugs me some,
But Grandma reminds me now and then
That Kwanzaa's about to come.

She whispers, "Umoja. What does it mean?"
I answer, "It's unity."
"And who, besides you," she presses on,
"Is in this community?"

And that's when I start to realize
We don't have to *love* each other,
But we must respect, protect, connect
Together each sister and brother.

African Trees

The maples on my avenue
Are bare and stiff with ice,
But I am filled with Kwanzaa
And I blink, astonished, twice…

They seem to melt before my eyes
And grow new leaves with ease,
Like African trees
Swaying in the breeze.

White egrets nest in them.
Black vultures rest in them.
African trees
Swaying in the breeze.

Ants form a train in them.
People store rain in them.
African trees
Swaying with the breeze.

Elephants munch on them.
Hyenas hunch "round them.
African trees
Swaying in the breeze.

Chimpanzees sleep in them,
Weaverbirds cheep in them,
African trees
Swaying to the breeze.

People use leaves from them
To make roofs and eaves from them,
African trees
Swaying with the breeze.

Men carve out masks from them,
Women form casks from them,
African trees
Swaying in the breeze.

Children make rafts from them
And splendid crafts from them,
African trees
Swaying to the breeze.

Bats chomp the fruits from them,
Grubs chow the roots of them,
African trrees
Swaying with the breeze.

Buffaloes wade beneath them.
Lions shade underneath them.
African trees
Swaying to the breeze.

Let's find a hive in them;
Bees are alive in them;
African trees
Swaying to the breeze.

Elms, chestnuts, maples,
Oaks – all of these –
Are African trees
Swaying in the breeze.

The Kids of Kwanzaa

Tariq and Shakira
Are clapping to the beat.
Nina and Tameeka
Kick their tiny feet.

Mike recalls the elders.
Marcus waves the flag.
Jasmine brings her presents
In a decorated bag.

Jesse feels creative.
Clare and Eve hold hands.
Tola's telling folk tales
About our native lands.

Theodore is laughing.
Nikki smiles wide.
James is filled with purpose.
Warren bursts with pride.

Kujichagulia

Kujichagulia
So much fun to say!
Kujichagulia,
It's the second day.
I will be responsible
For what I do and say.
I will set some noble goals
And reach those goals my way.

[4] *Kujichagulia is the second principle of Kwanzaa. It has to do with taking and keeping control of one's own life.*

Pearl and Roy, Girl and Boy

If I lived in Africa
And I were a girl,
My name might be Zahra (ZAH rah)
Or Umm (OOM) instead of Pearl.
Maybe I'd be Salma (SAHL mah),
Mandisa (mahn DEE sah), or Tatu (tah TOO),
Monifa (MOH nee fah), Aluna (ah LOO nah),
Doto (DOH toh), or Lulu (LOO loo).

If I lived in Africa
And I were a boy,
My name might be Sudi (soo dee),
Or Tor (TOOR) instead of Roy.
Mayba I'd be Simba (SEEM bah),
Masamba (mah SAHM bah), or Olu (oh LOO),
Jaja (JAH jah), Gogo (GOH goh), Juma (JOO mah),
Kondo (KOHN doh), or Badu (bah DOO)>

Aren't those names fantastic?
Which do you like the best?
I'll be from East Africa;
You be from the west.
We'll change our identities;
Won't it be such fun
To call each other different names,
Just 'til Kwanzaa's done?

[5] *The names, where they come from and they mean:*

Zahrah, East African, flower
Umm. North African, mother
Salma, East Africa, safe
Mandisa, South African, sweet
Tatu, East Africa, third born
Monifa, West Africa, "I have luck."
Aluna, East Africa, come here
Doto, East Africa, second twin
Lulu, East Africa, a pearl

Sudi, East Africa, luck
Tor, West Africa, king
Simba, East Africa, lion
Masamba, South Africa, leaves
Olu, West Africa, pre-eminent
Jaja, West Africa, honored
Gogo, South Africa, like his grandfather
Juma, East Africa, born on Friday
Kondo, East Africa, war
Badu, West Africa, tenth born

Kuumba

Hooray! Today's Kuumba,
Creativity.
And I decide to write a poem
About my family.

I decorate the border
With African designs
In golden, earthy colors
With black zig-zaggy lines.

I read it to my sister.
I read it to my brother.
My dad says, "You're amazing!"
"A genius," says my mother.

But Gramma sighs, exclaiming,
"Girl, I like your style!"
And, as tears run down her cheeks,
"How you make me smile!"

[6] *Kuumba (koo OOM bah) is the sixth principle of Kwanzaa and means "creativity."*

Gift for a Friend

What should I make my best friend?
What should I give her tonight?
"A store-bought present," Gramma says,
"Isn't exactly right.

"Call your creative powers;
Show off your wit and worth,
Like our African ancestors,
The greatest craftspeople on earth."

I think of their cloth and pottery
And baskets of woven reeds.
I think of their long looped earrings
And collars of colorful beads.

I measure elastic gold string
And thread on beads one by one,
Then tie the knots double to stay secure
When I am finally done.

Elveta adore my present.
Now I can't believe my eyes!
She gives me a beaded bracelet, too,
And it's the perfect size!

Listen to the Drums!

Listen to the
Listen to the African drums!
Rumbling in the garden
Like thunder when it comes.
Squirrels leap over puddles
And sparrows peck at crumbs
Near dried thistle
As they whistle
With the drums.

Listen to the
Listen to the African drums!
Tapping and a-rapping
As they cadence they repeat.
Musicians strum guitars
And play mbiras (em BEE rahs)* with their thumbs
As they imitate
The rhythms
Of the drums.

Listen to the
Listen to the African drums!
In my heart a-pounding
With purposeful resounding.
A gift from my ancestors,
So their echo it becomes
As I wrap my soul
Around the sound
Of drums!

Listen to the
Listen to the African drums!
Clear across my city
Where the Kwanzaa lights are pretty.
Every being shushes;
Hush, be quiet!
Here it comes…
Listen to the
Listen to the drums!

---

7 *mbira (em BEE rah) a thumb piano from Zimbabwe, made of eight flat
iron tines fixed to a wooden soundboard

The Kikombe Cup

Now it's time for sharing the kikombe (kee KHOM
bee) cup.
I tell my baby sister, "Just sip, don't drink it up."
Granddad gives the main speech from his trembling
lips.
Mama says her great-great-granny's name before she
sips.

Uncle Abe names ancestors we younger folks don't
know.
Cousin Fran gives tribute to her niece and Grand-Aunt
Flo.
Suddenly it's my turn; I whisper, like a prayerr,
The name of every friend and family member who is
there.

8

*The kikombe cup, or kikombe cha umoja (kee KHOM bee chah oo MOH jah)
is also called the "cup of togetherness" or the "unity cup." It is passed
around during the kutoa majina (koo TOH ah ma JEE nah). That is the part
of the Kwanzaa celebratation in which ancestors and African-American
ancestors are remembered.*

Kukumbuka

Kukumbuka, kukumbuka,
Calling our ancestors past.

Kukumbuka, kukumbuka,
May their spirits always last.

Kukumbuka, kukumbuka,
Some here, some across the sea.

Kukumbuka, kukumbuka,
Come, and stay alive in me!

[9] *Kukumbuka (koo KOOM boo kah) is calling the names of ancestors and
others born before us. This is done while the "cup of togetherness" is being
shared.*

Kwanzaa Girls

Ruby wraps a printed gele
Tightly 'round her hear
Harriet's dashiki lies,
Just ironed, on her bed.

Little Lila does some spins
To show off her new dress.
Rosa stomps around the room
And whines, "My hair's a mess!"

So Ruby combs and braids it
Neatly in cornrows
And fastens beads of red and black
And bright green as she goes.

Dad comes to the doorway
As lila does more twirls.
"Wow! Look at you!" he hugs them all,
"My perfect Kwanzaa girls."

[10] A gele (gay lay) is a woman's headwrap.
A dashiki (dah SHEE kee) is a loose blouse or loose long shirt.

One, Two, How Do You Do?

One, two,
How do you do?
I come from Ghana (GAH nah)
My name is Atsu (at SOO).
Father has gone to sea
In his canoe,
To bring back some fish
For the vegetable stew.
We'll eat with our fingers,
Is that fine with you?
Dipping our boiled yam balls
Called fufu (FOO FOO).

Three, four,
Come through my door.
I'll spread out a cowhide
Upon the earth floor
Of my Masai (muh SIGH) hut
That Mother has made.
We use it for sleeping
And also for shade.
I'm Shani (SHAH nee) of Kenya (KEN yah),
I'm glad you have stayed.
Here, share my milk gourd.
There's plenty. Have more.

Five, six,
One of my tricks
Is making a fire
With only two sticks.
I'm Toma (TOE mah), a Bushman
From dry desertlands.
My folks and I roam
Kalahari (kal uh HAHR ee) sands.
I eat hunted antelopes
And swift elands
And roots, nuts, and berries
That my mother picks.

Seven, eight,
Come watch me plait
Vegetable fibers
In rows tight and straight.
Ituri's (ee TOOR ee) the sight
Of my rainforest home.
My hut's leaf-covered
And shaped like a dome.
I am Onaso (oh NAH soh)
Who sleeps on the loam
Beneath the grand trees
That are bowed from rain's weight.

Nine, ten,
Down in the glen
Dunduns (DONE DONES) are beaten
By Yoruba (yo ROO bah) men.
I'm Olu (OH loo); my dancing folks
Travel in throngs
All over Nigeria (nigh JEER ee uh)
To hear the songs
Of goatskin drumheads
Connected by thongs,
"Talking" in their tongue
Again and again.

Oh, oh,
I am aglow,
Learning of Africa –
So much to know!
Each of my ancestors
Came from that place,
Strong in the spirit,
Brown in the face.
All of these children
In my storybook
Could be my kinfolk—
Just take a look.

Kwanzaa All The Year

Kwanzaa in the morning,
Kwanzaa in the night,
Kwanzaa when the rain falls,
Or sun is shining bright.

Kwanzaa when we're joyful,
Kwanzaa when there's fear,
Kwanzaa in the winter,
Kwanzaa all the year!

It is important to keep the Nguzo Saba (en GOO zoh SAH bah), Seven Principles of Kwanzaa, alive and in practice all year 'round.